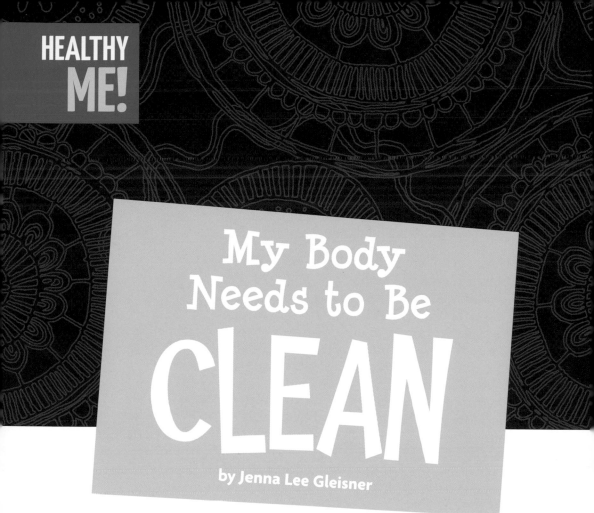

My Body Needs to Be CLEAN

by Jenna Lee Gleisner

amicus
high interest

Amicus High Interest is published by Amicus
P.O. Box 1329, Mankato, MN 56002
www.amicuspublishing.us

Library of Congress Cataloging-in-Publication Data
Gleisner, Jenna Lee, author.
  My body needs to be clean / by Jenna Lee Gleisner.
      pages cm. -- (Healthy me!)
  Summary: "Introduces the importance of keeping teeth, hands, hair, and
the body clean and proper ways to do so while offering safe, easy tips for
taking care of one's own body."-- Provided by publisher.
  Audience: Age 6.
  Audience: K to grade 3.
  Includes index.
  ISBN 978-1-60753-589-8 (hardcover) -- ISBN 978-1-60753-689-5 (pdf
ebook)
  1. Hygiene--Juvenile literature. 2. Baths--Juvenile literature. 3. Health--
Juvenile literature. I. Title.
  RA780.G57 2014
  613.4--dc23
                              2013046276

Photo Credits: Mike Flippo/Shutterstock Images, cover; Charles B. Ming
Onn/Shutterstock Images, 2, 11 (bottom left); Todd Gunkel/Thinkstock,
4; Lilya Espinosa/Shutterstock Images, 7; Thinkstock, 8; Shutterstock
Images, 11 (top left), 11 (middle left), 11 (middle right), 12, 19; JCJG
Photography/Shutterstock Images, 11 (top right), 22; Valentijn Tempels/
Shutterstock Images, 15; Vitalinko/Dreamstime.com, 16; Dejan Ristovski/
Thinkstock, 21

Produced for Amicus by The Peterson Publishing Company
and Red Line Editorial.

Designer Becky Daum
Printed in the United States of America
Mankato, MN
2-2014
PA10001
10 9 8 7 6 5 4 3 2 1

TABLE OF CONTENTS

4

GETTING DIRTY

Getting dirty is normal. It can be fun. But it is important to clean up. Why do we need to keep our bodies clean?

KEEPING CLEAN

We keep our bodies clean to look and smell nice. We also clean our bodies to get rid of **germs**. Germs can make us sick. They are too small to see.

8

STOPPING GERMS

Germs spread in the air. We can help keep germs from spreading too much. Cover your mouth and nose when you cough or sneeze. Throw away tissues and wash your hands afterward.

CLEAN HANDS

Germs get into our bodies. Too many germs can make us sick. Wash your hands many times each day. Wash them after going to the bathroom. Also wash them before you eat.

Healthy Hint

Wash your hands for at least 20 seconds. Time yourself. Sing the ABCs while you wash.

Wet your hands.

Add soap.

Scrub the backs of your
hands, fingers, and nails.

Rinse your hands
with clean water.

Dry your hands
on a clean towel.

CLEAN NAILS

Don't forget your fingernails. Wash under them when you wash your hands. Germs like to live under long nails. Trimming nails short keeps them clean.

CLEAN BODY

We touch many things each day. Germs can be on all of those things. You may need a bath or shower every day. It is important to wash your whole body. Warm, soapy water works best.

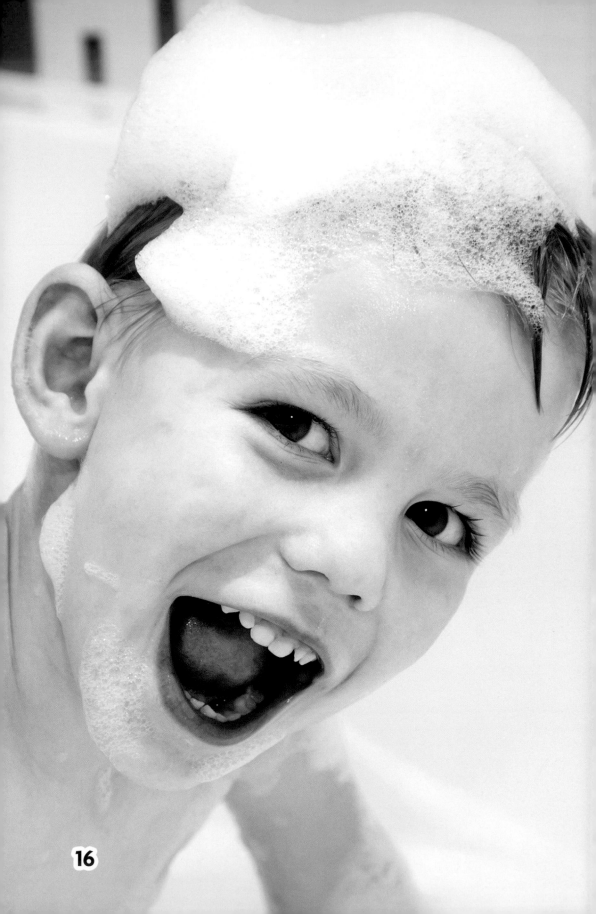

CLEAN HAIR

Get your whole **scalp** wet when you wash your hair. Rub the shampoo into your hair. Rub the suds into your scalp, too. This cleans your hair better.

Healthy Hint
Rinse your hair until all of the suds are gone. This washes away all of the shampoo and dirt.

CLEAN TEETH

Cleaning our mouths keeps us healthy, too. We need our teeth to chew food. Brushing our teeth cleans away **bacteria**. Bacteria can cause a **cavity**.

Healthy Hint

Brush your teeth at least two times each day. You do not need a lot of toothpaste. The size of a pea is enough.

KEEPING CLEAN

There are many ways to stay clean. We can keep our bodies clean every day. This helps stop the spread of germs. And it helps keep our bodies healthy!

GET STARTED TODAY

- Help stop germs from spreading by sneezing and coughing into a tissue or your elbow.

- Wash your hands after blowing your nose, using the bathroom, and before eating.

- Wash your hands for at least 20 seconds.

- Clean underneath your fingernails and keep them trimmed.

- Be sure to rub shampoo into your hair and scalp when washing your hair.

- Brush your teeth at least two times each day.

WORDS TO KNOW

bacteria – tiny living things that can be anywhere and make us sick

cavity – a hole in the tooth that forms when bacteria eats away at the tooth

germs – tiny living things that can cause disease

scalp – the skin that covers the top and back of your head

LEARN MORE

Books

Barraclough, Sue. *Wash and Clean*. Mankato, MN: Sea-to-Sea Publications, 2012.

Geis, Patricia. *Let's Wash Up!* New York: Alphabet Soup, 2010.

Web Sites

Did You Hear What Happened to the Tooth?
http://pbskids.org/sid//videoplayer.
html?pid=aPaID9jFbjMHumji6MQ_BYGqQ6DmKmwj
Watch and find out what happens to Ruth when she forgets to brush her teeth!

Teeth
http://kidshealth.org/kid/htbw/teeth-movie.html#cat118
Watch a video to learn more about your teeth!

Why Do I Need to Wash My Hands?
http://kidshealth.org/kid/talk/qa/wash_hands.html
Read more about why we need to keep our hands clean.

INDEX